Banff Travel Guide 2023-2024

The Ultimate Guide to Exploring Canada's Rocky Mountains

Bruce Terry

Bruce Terry

Copyright © 2023 Bruce Terry All rights reserved.

No part of this book may be reproduced, stored in a retrieval system, or transmitted in any form or by any means electronic, mechanical, photocopying, recording, scanning, or otherwise without the prior written permission of the publisher.

The work contained herein is the sole property of the author and may not be reproduced or copied in any form without express permission from the author. All information is provided as is, without any warranty of any kind, liability expressly disclaimed. The publisher and the author disclaim any liability for any loss, risk, or damage allegedly arising from the use, application, or interpretation of the content herein.

Bruce Terry

MAP OF BANFF

3 BANFF TRAVEL GUIDE 2023-2024

Bruce Terry

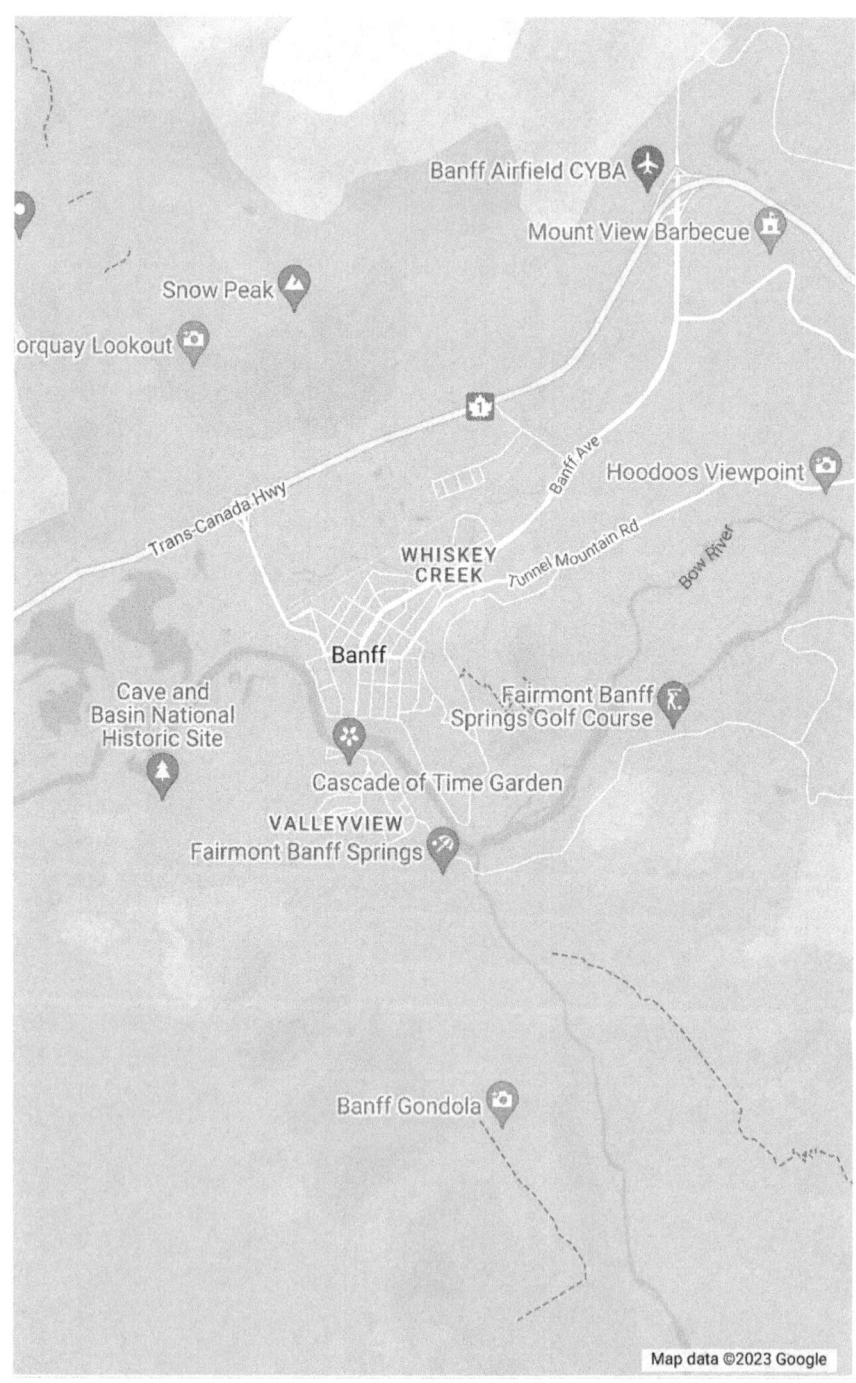

Bruce Terry

5 BANFF TRAVEL GUIDE 2023-2024

Bruce Terry

6 BANFF TRAVEL GUIDE 2023-2024

Bruce Terry

TABLE OF CONTENTS

MAP OF BANFF 3

INTRODUCTION 11

HISTORY AND CULTURAL SIGNIFICANCE 13

GEOGRAPHY AND CLIMATE 15

CHAPTER 1 19

PLANNING YOUR TRIP 19

- BEST TIME TO VISIT 19
- DURATION OF STAY 21
- ENTRY REQUIREMENTS AND PERMITS 23
- ACCOMMODATION OPTIONS 25
- TRANSPORTATION IN BANFF 27

CHAPTER 2 31

MUST-SEE ATTRACTIONS 31

- BANFF TOWNSITE 31

Banff Townsite Attractions: 31

Dining and Nightlife: 33

- LAKE LOUISE 34

Hiking: 36

Bruce Terry

- MORAINE LAKE 37

Exploring Moraine Lake: 38

Considerations for Safety: 39

- JOHNSTON CANYON 40
- BOW VALLEY PARKWAY 43

Animal Viewing: 44

- SULPHUR MOUNTAIN 45

Visitors' Recommendations 48

- ICEFIELDS PARKWAY 49

CHAPTER 3 53

OUTDOOR ACTIVITIES 53

- HIKING AND TREKKING TRAILS 53
- WILDLIFE SPOTTING 55
- CANOEING AND KAYAKING 58
- FISHING 61
- SKIING AND SNOWBOARDING 63
- MOUNTAIN BIKING 65
- CAMPING AND RVING 68

CHAPTER 4 71

Bruce Terry

CULTURAL EXPERIENCES 71

- INDIGENOUS HERITAGE AND CULTURAL CENTERS 71
- BANFF CENTRE FOR ARTS AND CREATIVITY 73
- BANFF PARK MUSEUMS 76
- CULTURAL EVENTS AND FESTIVALS 78

CHAPTER 5 81

DINING AND SHOPPING 81

- LOCAL CUISINE AND RESTAURANTS 81
- SHOPPING IN BANFF 83
- SOUVENIRS AND LOCAL CRAFTS 85

CHAPTER 6 89

PRACTICAL INFORMATION 89

- SAFETY TIPS AND GUIDELINES 89
- HEALTH AND MEDICAL SERVICES 92

Health Care: 92

- CURRENCY AND BANKING FACILITIES 95
- COMMUNICATION AND INTERNET ACCESS 97
- VISITORS INFORMATION CENTERS 99

Bruce Terry

Banff Visitor Information Centers: 100

CONCLUSION 102

Bruce Terry

INTRODUCTION

Welcome to Banff's stunning landscapes, where natural beauty knows no bounds and adventure awaits around every corner. Banff National Park, located in the heart of the Canadian Rockies, is an unparalleled playground for nature enthusiasts and avid adventurers. As we embark on the Banff Travel Guide 2023-2024 trip, we ask you to join us in discovering the secrets of this gorgeous destination.

Prepare to be enchanted by the raw charm of Banff, with its towering peaks, stunning blue lakes, and awe-inspiring glaciers. This thorough travel guide will serve as your guidebook, revealing the hidden treasures, must-see sights, and amazing experiences that await you in this alpine beauty.

Immerse yourself in the rich tapestry of outdoor activities available in Banff. Banff is a paradise for nature enthusiasts seeking serenity and adventure, with exhilarating hiking paths that lead to panoramic panoramas and thrilling animal encounters where you can observe secretive creatures in their native habitat. Whether you are a seasoned mountaineer or a casual hiker, a trail has been cut out specifically for you in this vast wilderness.

As you read through the pages of this travel book, you will come across a plethora of experiences that go beyond the limits of nature. With its picturesque streets, quirky stores, and diversified culinary scene, Banff's dynamic townsite entices. Indulge in the region's

Bruce Terry

delicacies, from hearty Canadian cuisine to international pleasures, and learn about the local customs and stories that have formed Banff into the cultural melting pot that it is today.

Furthermore, Banff is more than just a destination for outdoor enthusiasts and foodies. It's also a place for rest and renewal. As you embark on a journey of self-discovery and well-being, pamper yourself in magnificent hot springs, calm your senses in tranquil spas, and appreciate the serenity of the mountains.

We will take you through the ever-changing tapestry of activities and events that decorate this remarkable terrain as we navigate the seasons of Banff in 2023-2024. Banff promises a kaleidoscope of experiences that will leave an everlasting stamp on your soul, whether you seek the magic of winter sports, the awakening of spring blooms, the vibrancy of summer escapades, or the flaming hues of fall leaves.

So, let this Banff Travel Guide serve as your guide, inspiration, and key to discovering the enchantment that lies within this beautiful nature. Join us on this memorable voyage, where the spirit of adventure coexists with nature's tranquillity, and every moment carries the promise of wonder and discovery. Welcome to Banff, where dreams come true amid the breathtaking Canadian Rockies.

Bruce Terry

HISTORY AND CULTURAL SIGNIFICANCE

History is the study of historical events, particularly those concerning human society. It covers a wide range of topics, including political, social, economic, and cultural considerations. We learn about our ancestors' successes, failures, triumphs, and hardships by studying history. It enables us to comprehend our surroundings and to learn from the past to construct a better tomorrow.

One of the fundamental goals of history studies is to develop a better understanding of our common ancestry. It gives us a feeling of identity by connecting us to our ancestors and allowing us to understand the triumphs and hardships that past generations experienced. History also serves as a reminder of the cyclical nature of human experiences, highlighting recurring patterns and tendencies. We can make informed decisions and avoid repeating past mistakes if we recognize these tendencies.

Furthermore, history aids in the development of critical thinking and analytical skills. It teaches us to examine, assess, and interpret the information we have at our disposal. Historical analysis encourages us to consider many points of view and to question established narratives, resulting in a more sophisticated understanding of the intricacies inherent in human affairs. Furthermore, studying history allows us to cultivate empathy and compassion by immersing

Bruce Terry

ourselves in the lives of others, even those who lived in completely different times and places.

Cultural Importance: Culture can be broadly defined as a group's collective beliefs, values, conventions, traditions, and behaviors. Language, art, music, literature, religion, gastronomy, and social standards are all part of it. Culture shapes our identities, determines our conduct, and defines our sense of belonging.

A society's cultural relevance stems from its ability to offer individuals a framework for comprehending the world and their place in it. Culture influences our actions, decisions, and interactions with others. It gives us a sense of continuity, connecting us to the past while allowing us to adapt and evolve. Cultural practices and traditions are passed down from generation to generation, providing communities with a sense of stability and togetherness.

Culture is also important in creating diversity and building understanding among various groups of people. Each culture is a distinct expression of human intellect and imagination, providing significant insights into other ways of thinking and living. We may develop a more inclusive and harmonious global community by appreciating and accepting cultural differences.

Bruce Terry

Furthermore, artistic, musical, and literary manifestations provide a window into the human experience. They reflect a society's ideals, feelings, and values, allowing us to delve into the depths of human imagination and creativity. Whether antique sculptures, classical compositions, or literary masterpieces, cultural objects serve as enduring testaments to the richness and diversity of human culture.

GEOGRAPHY AND CLIMATE

Banff is located in a beautiful valley surrounded by towering mountains, making it a popular destination for outdoor enthusiasts and nature lovers. The village is located at an elevation of around 1,383 meters (4,537 feet) above sea level. The area is known for its rocky landscape, deep river basins, and glaciated summits.

The Canadian Rockies, which run from British Columbia to Alberta, are the most visible mountain range in the area. Mount Rundle, Cascade Mountain, and Mount Norquay are among the famous peaks near Banff. The area is also recognized for its beautiful lakes, such as Lake Louise and Moraine Lake, which are fed by glaciers and provide stunning views.

The village is located in Banff National Park, Canada's oldest national park, which encompasses an area of approximately 6,641 square kilometers (2,564 square miles). The park is a UNESCO World Heritage site that includes a variety of ecosystems such as alpine meadows, subalpine forests, and high mountain ranges. Elk, bighorn sheep, black bears, and grizzly bears live there, among other animals.

Climate: The subarctic climate of Banff is characterized by cold winters and pleasant summers. The high height and proximity to the Rocky Mountains have a significant impact on the climate. Here's a list of the seasons:

Winter (December to February): Banff's winters are bitterly cold, with temperatures frequently falling below freezing. The average temperature during the day ranges from -5°C (23°F) to -15°C (5°F). During this time, the town receives a substantial amount of snowfall, making it a winter sports enthusiast's paradise. Skiing, snowboarding, and snowshoeing are prominent winter sports in the area.

Spring (March to May): Although temperatures are gentler in the spring, snow may still be present at higher elevations. Temperatures during the day range from 5°C (41°F) to 10°C (50°F). The countryside comes alive with brilliant wildflowers as the snow melts, and hiking trails begin to open up.

Summer (June to August): Banff's summers are temperate and pleasant, with typical daily temperatures ranging from 15°C (59°F) to 25°C (77°F). Its peak tourist season, and people are flocking to the area to enjoy outdoor activities like hiking, mountain biking, and

Bruce Terry

animal watching. The days are long, allowing us plenty of time for exploring.

Autumn (September to November): Banff's autumn is distinguished by cool weather and a spectacular display of fall color. Temperatures during the day range from 5°C (41°F) to 15°C (59°F). The crowds begin to thin, making it a great opportunity to experience the park's quiet.

Bruce Terry

18 BANFF TRAVEL GUIDE 2023-2024

Bruce Terry

CHAPTER 1

PLANNING YOUR TRIP

- ### BEST TIME TO VISIT

Spring (March to May): As the snow melts, revealing lush green landscapes and blossoming wildflowers, spring in Banff gives a sense of regeneration. Temperatures begin to rise, with temperatures ranging from 5°C to 15°C (41°F to 59°F). While higher mountains may still have snow, lower levels provide great trekking options. The benefit of visiting Banff in the spring is that there are fewer people, making it an excellent time for serenity and calm exploration. However, be prepared for changing weather and carry suitable clothing layers.

Summer (June to August): Due to the mild weather and longer days, summer is the busiest tourist season in Banff. During the day, temperatures range from 15°C to 25°C (59°F to 77°F), while at night, they can dip to 5°C to 10°C (41°F to 50°F).

Hiking, biking, canoeing, and animal watching are just a few of the outdoor activities available throughout the summer months. The major sights of the park, including Lake Louise and Moraine Lake, are accessible, but they can get crowded, especially on weekends. If you plan to travel during this season, it is best to reserve your accommodations well in advance.

Bruce Terry

Fall (September to November): The landscapes in Banff are painted in bright hues of red, orange, and gold throughout the fall season. Temperatures begin to fall, with daytime temperatures ranging from 5°C to 15°C (41°F to 59°F) and nighttime temperatures plunging below freezing. Hiking and photography enthusiasts will enjoy the gorgeous fall foliage. In addition, when winter approaches, wildlife becomes more active. September and October are often less congested than the summer months, making them ideal for a relaxing vacation.

Winter (December to February): During the colder months, Banff transforms into a winter wonderland, enticing visitors with world-class skiing, snowboarding, ice climbing, and snowshoeing. Temperatures range from -5°C to -15°C (23°F to 5°F) but can get much colder.

Winter is a popular time to visit Banff due to the magnificent snow-covered landscapes, frozen lakes, and the opportunity to see the awe-inspiring Northern Lights. However, due to snowfall and avalanche risk, several roads, trails, and attractions may be blocked or have limited access. It's critical to keep an eye on the park's website for updates and make plans appropriately. In addition, because winter is considered the peak season for skiing, expect higher rates and larger crowds at famous ski resorts.

Bruce Terry

• DURATION OF STAY

Activities and Interests: Think about the activities and attractions you want to see in Banff. A longer stay is recommended if you want to visit prominent national parks, such as Banff National Park, Jasper National Park, or Yoho National Park. These parks are enormous, with several hiking paths, wildlife observation chances, and breathtaking vistas that demand plenty of time to fully appreciate.

Picturesque Drives: Banff is well-known for its picturesque drives, such as the Icefields Parkway, which connects Banff and Jasper. This drive might easily consume a whole day, especially if you intend to stop at vistas and sights along the way. Consider adding extra days to your plan to thoroughly appreciate these drives and explore the neighboring places.

Outdoor Activities: Hiking, mountain biking, canoeing, kayaking, skiing, snowboarding, and wildlife watching are just a few of the outdoor activities available in Banff. The length of your stay should correspond to the activities you want to do and the level of adventure you want. Hiking to alpine lakes, summiting mountain summits, or participating in winter sports will require extra time to completely immerse yourself in these activities.

Bruce Terry

Seasonal Considerations: The season in which you plan to visit can also influence the length of your stay. Banff is beautiful all year, yet each season offers something different. During the summer, for example, you can go hiking, see wildlife, and participate in numerous water activities. Skiing, snowboarding, and exploring frozen landscapes are all options in the winter. Remember that some activities are weather-dependent, so preparing ahead of time is vital.

Relaxation and exploration: In addition to outdoor activities, Banff boasts a wonderful ambiance with delightful restaurants, boutique stores, and local art galleries. You might want to set aside a couple of days to tour the area, rest in hot springs, or go for leisurely walks.

Given these considerations, here are some general recommendations for the length of your stay in Banff:

Short Trip: If you only have a few days to explore the town, see major destinations like Lake Louise and Moraine Lake, and participate in shorter treks or activities, a minimum of 2-3 days is recommended.

Moderate Trip: A stay of 4-6 days is appropriate for a more full experience. This time frame allows you to visit national parks, take scenic drives, participate in a range of outdoor activities, and relax in town.

Consider staying for a week or longer if you are a nature enthusiast, adventure seeker, or want to engage in significant trekking and exploring. This time will allow you to immerse yourself in the majesty of the Rockies, see lesser-known destinations, and develop a stronger relationship with nature.

• ENTRY REQUIREMENTS AND PERMITS

Passport and Visa Requirements: To enter Banff, you must have a valid passport that is valid for at least six months after your scheduled departure date. Visitors from certain countries may also be required to obtain a visa to enter Canada. It is critical to research the specific visa requirements for your country of citizenship. Before your journey, make sure you have the proper visa.

If you are a citizen of a visa-exempt nation, you may be required to apply for an Electronic Travel Authorization (eTA) to enter Canada. An eTA is a straightforward online application that requires a valid passport, an email account, and a minimal fee. To avoid last-minute hassles, apply for an eTA well in advance of your travel dates.

Travel Requirements for COVID-19: Due to the current COVID-19 pandemic, additional travel requirements may be in place to guarantee the safety of visitors and residents. Proof of immunization, negative COVID-19 testing, or mandated quarantine periods are examples of such criteria. Before traveling to Banff, it is critical to stay up to date on the latest travel recommendations and

Bruce Terry

restrictions issued by the Canadian government and local health authorities.

Banff National Park is located within Banff National Park, which is part of the Canadian National Parks system. To enter and enjoy the park as a visitor, you must purchase a National Park Entry Pass. The park's assets and services are preserved and maintained thanks to the pass payments. There are different types of passes available, including daily, yearly, and Discovery passes. The pass can be purchased online or at visitor centers and park gates.

Wilderness Permits: A wilderness permit is required if you intend to engage in backcountry camping, hiking, or overnight stays in designated wilderness regions inside Banff National Park. These permits aid in regulating the number of visitors in specific regions and preserving the park's natural beauty. It is critical to reserve your permit early, especially during high seasons, as availability may be restricted.

Fishing Licenses: With multiple lakes and rivers brimming with fish, Banff provides fantastic chances for fishing aficionados. A fishing license is required to fish lawfully in Banff National Park. The license costs go toward fishery conservation and habitat rehabilitation. Fishing licenses can be obtained online or at specified park locations.

Bruce Terry

• ACCOMMODATION OPTIONS

Luxury Hotels and Resorts: Banff is home to several world-class luxury hotels and resorts that offer unrivaled comfort and services. These hotels provide lavish rooms and suites, fine cuisine, spas, exercise centers, and concierge services. The Fairmont Banff Springs dubbed the "Castle in the Rockies," is a well-known landmark with a long history. The Rimrock Resort Hotel, the Post Hotel & Spa, and the Buffalo Mountain Lodge are among well-known possibilities.

Mid-Range Hotels & Motels: Banff has a variety of mid-range hotels and motels for guests looking for a blend of comfort and economy. These establishments offer pleasant rooms, friendly service, and handy locations. Popular choices include the Banff Aspen Lodge, Banff Caribou Lodge & Spa, and Banff Ptarmigan Inn, all of which provide a lovely stay at a reasonable price.

Cozy Bed & Breakfasts: Stay at one of Banff's beautiful bed and breakfasts for a more intimate and personalized experience. These facilities provide comfortable lodgings, home-cooked breakfasts, and friendly service. For their charming ambiance and attentive treatment, the Fox Hotel & Suites and the Poplar Inn are highly recommended.

Vacation rentals and condominiums: Vacation rentals and condominiums are great for families or bigger groups looking for

Bruce Terry

more space and freedom. Fully equipped kitchens, living areas, and numerous bedrooms are common features of these lodgings. Banff Lodging Company provides a wide range of vacation rentals and condos, including Hidden Ridge Resort and Tunnel Mountain Resort, to ensure a comfortable and home-like experience.

Hostels and inexpensive Accommodations: Banff has various hostels and inexpensive accommodations for budget-conscious guests and backpackers. These choices provide inexpensive dormitory-style accommodations, shared kitchens, and social areas, making them ideal for meeting other travelers. The HI-Banff Alpine Centre and Samesun Banff are popular options since they offer a comfortable and friendly atmosphere at a reasonable price.

Banff provides rustic cabins and lodges surrounded by nature for people looking for a true wilderness experience. These lodgings are frequently located in remote places, providing peace and solitude. Storm Mountain Lodge and Baker Creek Mountain Resort, for example, provide quiet cottages with breathtaking views, allowing you to escape from the outside world and immerse yourself in the majesty of Banff.

Bruce Terry

• TRANSPORTATION IN BANFF

Getting to Banff:

a. *By Air:* Calgary International Airport (YYC), located roughly 145 kilometers (90 miles) east of Banff, is the closest international airport. To get to Banff, you can rent a car, ride a shuttle, or charter a private transfer from the airport.

b. *By Car:* The Trans-Canada Highway (Highway 1) connects Banff to the rest of the country. The park is located roughly 1.5 hours west of Calgary and may be reached by driving through the scenic Rocky Mountains.

Banff Transportation Options:

a. *Car Rental:* Renting a car gives you the most freedom and convenience when exploring Banff National Park. In Calgary and Banff, several car rental firms offer a variety of vehicle options to fit your needs. In particular, during the busiest times of the year, reservations should be made in advance.

b. *Roam Transit:* Roam Transit is an excellent public transportation system in Banff. This service offers bus service inside Banff as well as shuttle services to famous park locations such as Lake Louise and the Banff Gondola.

Bruce Terry

c. *Taxis:* and ride-sharing services such as Uber and Lyft are accessible in Banff, providing an alternate form of transportation within the town and its close surroundings.

d. *Bicycles:* Banff is a bike-friendly destination, and bicycles may be rented from a variety of stores in town. Cycling is an excellent way to explore the park's gorgeous roads and trails, particularly during the warmer months.

Banff and the Surrounding Areas:

a. *Banff Town:* Banff is a small town that is readily walkable. Most lodgings are within walking distance of numerous activities, including restaurants, shops, and galleries.

b. *Roam Transit:* As previously stated, Roam Transit operates throughout Banff and provides shuttle services to popular locations. These shuttles are especially useful for visiting Lake Louise, Moraine Lake, and the Banff Gondola because they provide hassle-free transportation and eliminate the need to find parking.

c. *Sightseeing excursions:* Several tour companies provide guided sightseeing excursions in Banff and the surrounding areas. These excursions frequently include transportation, competent guides, and visits to popular locations, resulting in an enjoyable and educational experience.

Bruce Terry

d. *National Park Pass:* A valid park pass, which can be obtained at the park's entrance gates, visitor centers, or online, is required to explore Banff National Park. The park's picturesque roads, hiking trails, and attractions are all accessible with the pass.

Bruce Terry

30 BANFF TRAVEL GUIDE 2023-2024

Bruce Terry

CHAPTER 2

MUST-SEE ATTRACTIONS

• BANFF TOWNSITE

Getting There:

Banff Townsite is located in the Canadian province of Alberta. Calgary International Airport (YYC), the nearest major international airport, is roughly 90 minutes distant by vehicle. To get to Banff, you can rent a car, use a shuttle, or take public transit from the airport. Alternatively, tour organizations provide planned transportation to and from Banff.

Banff Townsite Attractions:

2.1. *Banff Avenue:* Banff Avenue, the main thoroughfare of Banff Townsite, is lined with a variety of stores, galleries, restaurants, and lodgings. Take a stroll down the avenue to take in the vibrant ambiance of the town and explore its distinctive boutiques and souvenir shops.

2.2. *Banff Park* Museum National Historic Site: This museum, located on Banff Avenue, is a must-see for nature and history buffs. It houses a large collection of preserved wildlife specimens that provide insight into the area's great biodiversity as well as the history of Banff National Park.

Bruce Terry

2.3. *Bow Falls:* Located just a short distance from Banff Townsite, Bow Falls provides a magnificent setting for relaxation and appreciation of the region's natural splendor. A picturesque walk down the Bow River will take you right to the falls.

2.4. *Cave and Basin National Historic Site*: hear about the history of Banff National Park at this historic site, where you may visit an underground cave and hear about the hot springs that inspired the park's creation. There are also explanatory exhibits and guided tours at the site.

2.5. *Banff Gondola:* Take a ride on the Banff Gondola for an incredible panoramic view of Banff and its surrounding mountains. The gondola transports you to Sulphur Mountain's summit, where you can enjoy beautiful views, hiking trails, and a tourist center.

Outdoor Recreation:

3.1. *Hiking:* Banff National Park has a variety of hiking paths to accommodate all levels of experience. You may experience breathtaking landscapes, alpine meadows, and pristine lakes on short walks or multi-day excursions. Hikes through Johnston Canyon, Lake Minnewanka, and the Plain of Six Glaciers are popular.

3.2. *Species Observation:* Banff is home to a wide variety of species, including elk, deer, bighorn sheep, and bears. To enhance your chances of seeing these wonderful species in their native habitat, take a wildlife trip or visit the park with a professional guide.

3.3. *Canoeing and Kayaking:* Rent a canoe or kayak to enjoy the peacefulness of Banff's lakes and rivers. Lake Louise and Moraine Lake are especially popular kayaking destinations, with magnificent turquoise waters surrounded by majestic mountains.

3.4. *Skiing and Snowboarding*: During the winter, Banff transforms into a winter wonderland, drawing skiers and snowboarders from all over the world. Mount Norquay, Sunshine Village, and Lake Louise Ski Resort are the three major ski resorts in the area, with a variety of slopes for all ability levels.

Dining and Nightlife:

Banff Townsite has a diverse culinary scene with a wide range of dining options to suit every taste and budget. From quiet cafés and pubs to upmarket restaurants, you may sample a wide range of cuisines, including Canadian, foreign, and regional specialties. After supper, enjoy the town's vibrant nightlife, which includes clubs, pubs, and live music venues that stay open late.

Accommodations:

Banff Townsite has a variety of lodging options, from luxury resorts and boutique hotels to budget-friendly hostels and campers. Whether you want a cozy mountain lodge or a sophisticated hotel,

Bruce Terry

Banff has accommodations to meet your needs. Booking rooms well in advance is recommended, especially during peak tourist seasons.

• LAKE LOUISE

Location and Directions: Lake Louise is located about 180 kilometers (112 miles) west of Calgary, Alberta. Flying into Calgary International Airport and then hiring a car for the gorgeous 2-hour trip to Lake Louise is the most convenient way to get there. Alternatively, you can use a shuttle service or public transit.

Lake Louise is a year-round attraction, with each season presenting its distinct charm and activities.

Summer (June to August) is the most popular time to visit, with mild temperatures, beautiful skies, and the chance to explore the lake's hiking trails, kayaking, and canoeing. Fall (September to November) offers stunning autumn colors, fewer visitors, and perfect hiking conditions. Winter (December to February) transforms the environment into a winter wonderland, drawing people who come to ski, snowboard, and ice skate. Spring (March through May) brings warmer weather, the opportunity to see wildlife, and the blooming of gorgeous wildflowers.

Accommodation alternatives: Lake Louise has a variety of lodging alternatives to suit every traveler's needs. Here are a few interesting possibilities, ranging from luxurious mountain resorts to quiet lodges and budget-friendly hotels:

The Fairmont Chateau. Lake Louise: A world-famous luxury hotel with breathtaking lake views and posh amenities.

Deer Lodge is a lovely historic lodge with rustic elegance and pleasant rooms.

Lake Louise Inn: A cozy and reasonably priced motel with a variety of room options and on-site services.

Baker Creek Mountain Resort: A natural hideaway with log cabins and cottages.

Attractions to See:

a. *Lake Louise*: The main attraction, with its hypnotic turquoise waters and the majestic Victoria Glacier in the background. Explore the shoreline, hire a canoe, or simply enjoy the breathtaking scenery.

b. *Moraine Lake:* Moraine Lake is a short drive from Lake Louise and is another must-see attraction. Its vivid blue-green waters are extremely magnificent, flanked by high mountains.

c. *Plain of Six Glaciers track:* A popular hiking track that leads to a teahouse with panoramic views of glaciers.

Bruce Terry

d. *Lake Agnes Trail:* This path leads to the lovely Lake Agnes Tea House, which is perched above Lake Louise. Take a well-deserved break and take in the breathtaking environment.

e. *The Icefields Parkway:* A scenic drive from Lake Louise to Jasper that offers breathtaking views of glaciers, waterfalls, and snow-capped peaks.

Hiking:

Lake Louise is a hiker's paradise, with paths for hikers of all skill levels. There's something for everyone, from relaxing strolls around the lake to strenuous alpine hikes.

b. *Canoeing and Kayaking*: Rent a canoe or kayak to see Lake Louise from the water and see the surrounding mountain peaks reflected in its pure waters.

c. *Skiing and Snowboarding:* Lake Louise Ski Resort offers world-class downhill skiing and snowboarding during the winter months. Enjoy the manicured slopes, breathtaking views, and powder-filled bowls.

d. *Wildlife Viewing:* While exploring the trails or driving around the park, keep an eye out for wildlife such as elk, deer, moose, and even grizzly bears. Keep a safe distance from them and observe them properly.

Bruce Terry

Lake Louise has a wide range of dining alternatives, from informal cafes to expensive restaurants serving local and international cuisine. Don't pass up the opportunity to enjoy Canadian favorites like poutine and foods flavored with maple syrup. There are also various shops and boutiques in the hamlet where you can buy souvenirs, outdoor gear, and locally-made crafts.

- **MORAINE LAKE**

Getting There:

Moraine Lake is located in Alberta, Canada, about 14 kilometers (8.7 miles) southeast of the town of Lake Louise. The closest significant international airport is Calgary International Airport (YYC), which is situated around 183 kilometers (114 miles) away. Visitors can access Moraine Lake by driving from Calgary via the Trans-Canada Highway (Highway 1) and the Icefields Parkway (Highway 93). Shuttle services are also available from Lake Louise, providing a convenient and environmentally responsible mode of transportation.

The greatest time to visit Moraine Lake is during the summer months (June to September) when the lake thaws and turns a beautiful turquoise color due to the glacial rock flour suspended in the water. However, this means more people, particularly during July and August. Consider visiting in early June or September for a more tranquil experience. Moraine Lake becomes a winter paradise

Bruce Terry

in the winter, with frozen lake surfaces and snow-covered mountains, drawing winter sports lovers and photographers.

Weather and Clothing: Because the weather in Banff is so unpredictable, it's important to dress in layers and be prepared for changing conditions. Summer temperatures might range from 10°C to 25°C (50°F to 77°F), so bring a thick jacket or sweater for chilly evenings. Temperatures can dip well below freezing in the winter, so bring suitable winter apparel, such as insulated jackets, caps, gloves, and thick boots.

Exploring Moraine Lake:

Moraine Lake is well-known for its postcard-worthy landscape, and there are various ways to enjoy it:

a. *Rockpile Trail:* A short and simple climb that provides a panoramic view of Moraine Lake from a viewpoint atop a tiny hill.

b. *Larch Valley-Sentinel Pass Trail*: This moderate to difficult hike rewards hikers with beautiful views of the valley, alpine meadows, and glaciers.

c. *Canoeing and Kayaking*: From the Moraine Lake Lodge, rent a canoe or kayak and paddle across the magnificent blue waters flanked by towering mountains. It's a peaceful and magical experience that gives you a new perspective on the lake's splendor.

d. *Photography:* Moraine Lake is a photographer's dream location. Capture the shifting colors of the lake throughout the day, with the finest light for photography coming in the morning and late afternoon. Remember to bring your tripod for those steady long-exposure photographs.

e. animals Spotting: Keep a look out for animals such as black bears, grizzly bears, elk, deer, and numerous bird species in the vicinity. Keep a safe distance from them and respect their natural habitat.

Moraine Lake has visitor facilities such as parking lots, restrooms, a café, and a gift store to guarantee a comfortable visit. It's critical to arrive early in the day because parking is limited and lots fill up rapidly, especially during peak season.

Considerations for Safety:

It is critical to consider safety when visiting Moraine Lake:

a. *Bear Aware:* Because this is a bear country, be familiar with bear safety measures, carry bear spray, and make noise when hiking to prevent unexpected wildlife.

b. *Stay on Designated Trails:* To protect the fragile alpine ecosystem and avoid destroying vegetation, stay on designated trails.

c. *Monitor Weather Conditions:* Be aware of shifting weather patterns and be prepared for rapid changes in weather by carrying suitable gear.

Bruce Terry

d. *Leave No Trace*: Respect the environment by packing out all waste and following the Leave No Trace principles to maintain Moraine Lake's natural beauty for future generations.

• JOHNSTON CANYON

History of Johnston Canyon:

The canyon was named after a Scottish-born explorer called John Johnston, who found it in the late 1800s. The area immediately became popular with tourists, resulting in the development of well-maintained pathways and infrastructure. Today, Johnston Canyon is one of the most recognizable natural features of Banff National Park.

Getting There:

Johnston Canyon is easily accessible from Banff, which is around 25 kilometers distant. Banff can be reached by automobile, shuttle service, or public transit. The canyon is about a 30-minute drive from Banff along the picturesque Bow Valley Parkway (Highway 1A). Alternatively, throughout the summer, shuttle services from Banff to Johnston Canyon are available.

Best Time to Visit:

Johnston Canyon is beautiful in all seasons, each with its distinct charm. Because of the nice weather, rich foliage, and full-flowing

Bruce Terry

• BOW VALLEY PARKWAY

Getting There:

The Bow Valley Parkway starts on the Trans-Canada Highway about 5 kilometers (3.1 miles) west of Banff. The parkway is readily accessible by automobile or via scheduled trips. It's a short drive to the parkway's entrance if you're staying in Banff or Lake Louise.

a. *Johnston Canyon:* One of the most popular sites along the Bow Valley Parkway, Johnston Canyon provides a mesmerizing stroll through a limestone canyon replete with stunning waterfalls and turquoise pools. The route is well-kept and has catwalks and bridges that enable tourists to see the canyon from different perspectives.

b. *Castle Mountain:* Enjoy beautiful views of Castle Mountain as you travel along the parkway. This renowned mountain rises magnificently from the surrounding countryside and offers fantastic photographic opportunities.

c. *Baker Creek:* About halfway between Banff and Lake Louise, Baker Creek is a lovely area for a picnic or a short trek. The stream flows through a beautiful valley, and there's a lovely lodge where you may eat or stay overnight.

d. *Morant's Curve:* This well-known viewpoint provides a breathtaking perspective of the Canadian Pacific Railway as it passes through the Bow River Valley. Morant's Curve is especially

Bruce Terry

picturesque at dawn and sunset when the railroad lines curve smoothly across the spectacular mountain backdrop.

Animal Viewing:

The Bow Valley Parkway is well-known for its animal sightings, which allow visitors to get up close and personal with a variety of species. Keep a watch out for elk, deer, black bears, and, on rare occasions, grizzly bears. Always keep a safe distance and never approach or feed the animals. For recording these spectacular moments, binoculars and a camera with a zoom lens come in useful.

Hiking and Outdoor Activities:

The Bow Valley Parkway connects to several hiking paths appropriate for hikers of all experience levels. Among the prominent alternatives are:

a. *Peyto Lake:* Although Peyto Lake is not immediately accessible from the Bow Valley Parkway, it is a short drive away. The route to the lookout provides a breathtaking picture of the lake's vivid blue waters against the background of the surrounding highlands.

b. *Protection Mountain and Mount Edith:* These modest treks provide breathtaking views and an opportunity to immerse yourself in nature. The pathways highlight the park's varied vegetation and wildlife, which include wildflowers and bird species.

Bruce Terry

c. *Bow Valley Parkway Bike Ride:* Cyclists may take a leisurely ride around the parkway at their speed, soaking in the picturesque splendor. The speed restriction is lower than on the Trans-Canada Highway, which makes riding safer and more fun.

d. *Timing:* The Bow Valley Parkway is open all year, however, certain portions may shut throughout the winter due to weather conditions. Before you go, check for road closures and current conditions.

e. *Wildlife Safety:* Be aware of the presence of wildlife and maintain a safe distance. Grizzly spray is recommended, particularly while trekking in grizzly areas. Make yourself familiar with bear safety procedures.

f. *Photography:* Don't forget to bring your camera to capture the breathtaking scenery. The golden hours (sunrise and sunset) provide photographers with beautiful lighting conditions.

g. *Plan Your Route:* For a complete Rockies experience, combine a trip along the Bow Valley Parkway with excursions to surrounding sights such as Lake Louise, Moraine Lake, and the town of Banff.

- **SULPHUR MOUNTAIN**

Sulphur Mountain is one of the most recognizable and stunning sights in Alberta, Canada's Banff National Park. This majestic mountain gives tourists breathtaking views of the surrounding

Bruce Terry

Canadian Rockies and an amazing outdoor experience. In this travel guide, we will look at the different sights and activities that Sulphur Mountain has to offer, as well as practical advice to help you make the most of your stay.

How to Get There

Sulphur Mountain is readily accessible from Banff, which is around 5 kilometers distant. Visitors may drive themselves or use the Banff Gondola, a popular form of transit to the peak.

If you prefer to drive, travel the Trans-Canada Highway (Highway 1) to Banff and then take the Mountain Avenue exit. Continue on Mountain Avenue until you reach the Banff Gondola base station parking lot. A short stroll will take you to the gondola launching point.

The Banff Gondola is a simple and picturesque method to reach Sulphur Mountain's peak. The gondola trip lasts around eight minutes and offers breathtaking views of the surrounding environment. Tickets may be bought at the base station or in advance online.

Summit of Sulphur Mountain

Sulphur Mountain's top, at 2,281 meters (7,486 feet), provides stunning views of Banff National Park and the surrounding Rocky

Bruce Terry

Mountains. The following are some of the summit's highlights and activities:

Observation Decks: Enjoy the breathtaking views from the several observation decks strategically placed around the peak. These terraces provide unrestricted views of the surrounding hills, valleys, and Banff town.

Sulphur Mountain Boardwalk: Walk along the ridge of Sulphur Mountain on the boardwalk. This interpretive walk provides visitors with information on the surrounding flora, wildlife, and geology, helping them to have a better knowledge of the natural environment.

Cosmic Ray Station: Tour the historic Cosmic Ray Station, which was erected in the 1950s as a meteorological station. Learn about the station's scientific studies and the significance it played in comprehending cosmic rays.

Summit Ridge Trail: The Sulphur Mountain Summit Ridge Trail is a somewhat difficult trek for those looking for a more immersive outdoor experience. This 5.5-kilometer (3.4-mile) trek takes hikers through gorgeous alpine scenery and rewards them with breathtaking vistas along the way.

Dining & Shopping: Indulge in a delicious meal or pick up a keepsake at the summit's restaurants and gift stores. Enjoy lunch

Bruce Terry

with a view or purchase one-of-a-kind souvenirs to remember your visit to Sulphur Mountain.

Visitors' Recommendations

Dress in layers: Because the weather at the peak may be unpredictable, it's best to layer up to suit shifting temperatures.

Wear durable and comfy shoes: If you wish to trek the Summit Ridge Trail or explore the boardwalk, wear sturdy and comfortable shoes.

Check the weather prediction: Before going to Sulphur Mountain, be sure to check the weather forecast to guarantee good visibility and hiking conditions.

When to go: The Mountain may become busy during high tourist seasons, so go early in the day or on weekdays for a more peaceful experience.

Bring your camera: The views from Sulphur Mountain are very magnificent, so bring your camera to capture the amazing surroundings.

Bruce Terry

• ICEFIELDS PARKWAY

The Icefields Parkway, commonly known as Highway 93, connects the town of Lake Louise in Banff National Park to Jasper National Park and extends for 232 kilometers (144 miles). It is generally regarded as one of the world's most magnificent drives, with breathtaking vistas of snow-capped mountains, clean lakes, and unspoiled nature.

Getting There:

The Icefields Parkway may be reached through two major gateways: Calgary (about 180 kilometers east of Banff) and Edmonton (about 365 kilometers northeast of Banff). Both cities feature international airports and automobile rental agencies. Well-maintained roadways connect both cities to Banff National Park.

The Icefields Parkway is accessible all year, although the ideal time to come is during the summer months (June to September) when the weather is nice and the road conditions are good. However, if you like winter activities such as skiing or snowshoeing, the parkway also provides breathtaking views throughout the winter season.

a. *Lake Louise:* Begin your adventure with the famed Lake Louise, noted for its emerald waters and spectacular mountain background. Explore the beach, go canoeing, or trek to the Lake Agnes Tea House.

Bruce Terry

b. *Peyto Lake:* Peyto Lake is a short drive from Lake Louise and has vibrant blue waters as well as spectacular panoramic views from a viewpoint accessible through a short climb.

c. *Columbia Icefield:* This immense expanse of ice encompasses over 200 square kilometers (77 square miles) and is one of North America's greatest ice fields. For an unforgettable experience, take a guided tour of the Athabasca Glacier or visit the Columbia Icefield Skywalk.

d. *Athabasca Falls:* Experience nature's raw strength as the Athabasca River plunges down a tight valley, forming a stunning cascade. Well-kept paths give fantastic photographic opportunities.

e. *Sunwapta Falls:* Sunwapta Falls, located just north of the Columbia Icefield, has spectacular cascades surrounded by high peaks. Both the higher and lower falls are accessible through a short trek.

f. *Jasper National Park:* You'll enter Jasper National Park as you near the northern end of the Icefields Parkway. Explore the picturesque town of Jasper, go animal watching, and participate in sports including hiking, fishing, and bicycling.

Bruce Terry

Activities and trekking:

The Icefields Parkway provides several chances for outdoor activities and trekking. There's something for every level of explorer, from short walks to multi-day adventures. In Jasper National Park, prominent routes include the Parker Ridge Trail, Wilcox Pass Trail, and the famed Skyline Trail.

Services and Facilities: There are various visitor centers, campsites, picnic spaces, and petrol stations along the Icefields Parkway. However, since services are restricted in certain locations, it is critical to prepare ahead and bring extra supplies.

Wildlife and safety: Bears, elk, mountain goats, and bighorn sheep may be seen in Banff National Park, as well as a variety of other animals. To guarantee your safety and the well-being of the animals, keep a safe distance, never feed the animals, and obey park standards.

Photography Tips: The Icefields Parkway offers several picture options. Carry your camera and capture the beauty of the scenery at various times of the day. Sunrise and dusk provide magnificent lighting conditions, and clear mornings often provide stunning reflections on the lakes.

Bruce Terry

52 BANFF TRAVEL GUIDE 2023-2024

may take in the breathtaking views of Banff National Park, including Mount Assiniboine. Allow for a whole day and come prepared with the necessary equipment and food.

Hiking & Trekking Tips in Banff:

Before starting, check trail conditions and weather predictions.

Wear layers and suitable footwear.

Carry necessary equipment such as maps, a compass, bear spray, and enough water.

Respect animals and abide by park rules.

Leave no trace: pack away all waste to reduce your environmental effect.

For a safe and instructive experience, consider hiring a guide or attending a guided tour.

- ## WILDLIFE SPOTTING

Banff National Park's Wildlife: Banff National Park is home to a diverse range of wildlife, including big animals, birds, and smaller species. Grizzly bears, black bears, elk, moose, wolves, bighorn sheep, mountain goats, and the elusive mountain lions are among the park's renowned wildlife. Birds such as bald eagles, ospreys, and golden eagles may be seen flying over the sky, while beavers and pikas flourish in Banff's unique ecosystems.

Bruce Terry

Best Seasons for Wildlife Spotting: To enhance your chances of seeing wildlife, visit Banff National Park during the appropriate seasons. Spring and autumn are especially gratifying since animals are more active during these transitional seasons. Spring affords the chance to witness young animals, while October delivers the sight of elk and deer rutting. However, animals may be seen in Banff all year, so arrange your trip around your interests.

Tips for Wildlife Viewing:

a) *Respect Wildlife:* It is important to keep a reasonable distance from wildlife. Approaching or feeding them might be dangerous to their health and safety. For a closer view, use binoculars, telephoto lenses, or spotting scopes.

b) *Be Quiet and Patient:* Loud sounds or quick movements might startle wildlife. Allow animals to perform normally while being calm and patient.

c) *Time of Day:* Wildlife activity is most active in the early morning and late evening. Many creatures are more active during the colder hours, which increases your chances of seeing them.

d) *Lake Minnewanka:* This lovely lake provides an opportunity to see bighorn sheep, elk, and even the odd bear. Take a wildlife excursion or explore the hiking trails in the region for a closer look.

e) *Bow Valley Parkway:* This picturesque route is well-known for animal observations. Drive gently and watch for wildlife such as wolves, elk, and black bears.

f) *Icefields Parkway:* This well-known roadway provides breathtaking scenery and good animal viewing chances. Along the way, keep a lookout for mountain goats, bighorn sheep, and bears.

g) *Johnston Canyon*: Known for its stunning waterfalls, this area is also home to animals such as black bears and birds.

h) *Vermilion Lakes:* These lakes, located just outside of Banff, attract a variety of waterfowl and bird species, making it an excellent place for birding.

Guided Wildlife Tours:

Consider attending a guided wildlife tour for a more in-depth wildlife experience. Knowledgeable guides may give insights into animal behavior, make your visit safer, and help you better appreciate the Banff environment.

Considerations for Safety: While animal interactions may be thrilling, it is important to consider safety. Stay on approved routes, bring bear spray, and educate yourself with Parks Canada's animal safety recommendations. You may have a safe and wonderful wildlife adventure if you respect the animals and their environments.

Bruce Terry

• CANOEING AND KAYAKING

Rivers in Banff:

Banff National Park is home to several beautiful rivers ideal for canoeing and kayaking. Here are some noteworthy alternatives:

a. *Lake Louise:* With its turquoise waters and surrounding snow-capped peaks, Lake Louise is a must-see for paddlers. Rent a canoe or kayak and explore the quiet waterways, soaking in the beautiful surroundings and perhaps seeing animals.

b. *Moraine Lake:* Moraine Lake, known for its bright blue hue and magnificent valley vistas, offers a wonderful setting for paddlers. While admiring the surrounding mountains, take a peaceful paddle around the glacier-fed lake.

c. *Bow River:* The Bow River runs through Banff, providing a range of paddling opportunities. The Bow River offers a variety of exploring options, from quiet parts appropriate for novices to more demanding stretches for expert kayakers.

d. *Spray Lakes:* The Spray Lakes, located just outside Banff National Park, provide a beautiful environment for kayaking. This location is ideal for kayakers and canoeists looking for a more private experience, with crystal-clear waterways and a quiet ambiance.

Bruce Terry

Equipment and Rentals:

To truly enjoy your canoeing or kayaking excursion in Banff, you must have the proper equipment. While some guests may prefer to carry their equipment, rentals are easily accessible in Banff. These rental establishments provide a variety of alternatives, such as canoes, kayaks, paddles, and safety equipment. Before you go, be sure you've chosen a trustworthy rental company and that the equipment is in excellent working order.

Precautions:

When participating in any water-based activity, safety should always be a primary consideration. Consider the following safety considerations for a fun and safe experience:

a. *Wear a Personal Flotation Device (PFD):* While on the water, always wear a properly fitted PFD. It is critical for your safety, particularly if you are a weak swimmer.

b. *Examine Weather and Water Conditions:* Before going on your journey, examine the weather forecast and be aware of any possible risks, such as high winds or quickly changing water levels.

c. *Notify Others:* Inform others about your intended itinerary and approximate return time. This guarantees that someone is aware of your whereabouts and may notify authorities if required.

Bruce Terry

d. *Paddle with a Buddy:* Paddle with a partner or a group whenever feasible. It not only improves safety but also adds to the overall pleasure of the event.

e. *Be Bear-Aware*: Bears live in Banff National Park. Familiarize yourself with bear safety procedures and carry bear spray as a preventive measure.

Restrictions and Permits:

Be mindful of the restrictions and permission requirements while planning your canoeing or kayaking expedition in Banff. Some rivers may have unique regulations, such as limitations on powered boats or designated paddling zones. Additionally, to access specific lakes or rivers inside Banff National Park, admission fees and permits may be necessary. Up-to-date information on permits and restrictions may be found on the Parks Canada website or in the park's information centers.

Best Time to Visit:

The canoeing and kayaking season in Banff usually starts in late spring and lasts until early October. The optimum time to visit is determined by your tastes and the waterway you choose to explore. Summer months (June to August) are ideal for kayaking because of the beautiful weather and extended daylight hours. If you prefer fewer visitors, travel during the shoulder seasons of spring or autumn, when the landscape is equally magnificent.

• FISHING

Banff Fishing Locations:

Banff National Park has a plethora of fishing spots, each with its own distinct angling experience. Listed below are some of the most well-liked spots:

a. *Bow River:* Flowing through Banff, the Bow River is famous for its excellent fly fishing. It is home to brown trout, rainbow trout, and whitefish, giving fishermen a variety of options.

b. *Lake Minnewanka:* This massive glacial lake is a popular fishing site. It provides the opportunity to capture lake trout (char), mountain whitefish, and bull trout. Anglers may reach the lake by boat or by land.

c. *Moraine Lake:* Surrounded by breathtaking mountain peaks, Moraine Lake is not only aesthetically appealing but also an excellent fishing spot. It is well-recognized for its brook and rainbow trout populations.

d. *Vermilion Lakes:* Located just outside of Banff, Vermilion Lakes is a network of small lakes with exceptional trout, pike, and whitefish fishing. It has easy access and beautiful views.

e. *Fishing restrictions:* It is essential to follow fishing restrictions to protect the survival of the fisheries in Banff National Park. Here are some important things to keep in mind:

f. *Fishing License:* Anglers aged 16 and over must have a current Alberta sportfishing license, which is available online or via approved merchants.

g. *Fishing Seasons*: Fishing is permitted in Banff from late spring through autumn. Specific dates and seasonal closures are available on the Parks Canada website.

h. *Limits & Catch-and-Release:* Each fish species has daily catch limits, and some places impose catch-and-release rules. It is essential to be aware of these constraints and follow the rules.

i. *Fishing Gear:* To avoid fish injury, the use of barbless hooks and artificial lures is suggested. For precise gear requirements for each fishing area, see the rules.

Tips for a Successful Fishing Trip:

To get the most out of your fishing trip in Banff, consider the following:

a. *Hiring a Tour Guide:* Hiring a professional fishing guide may substantially improve your experience if you are new to fishing or unfamiliar with the region. They may provide you with information on local procedures, venues, and laws.

b. *Study and Planning:* Before your trip, do some study on the fishing sites, current circumstances, and species you want to catch. This information will assist you in selecting the appropriate equipment and approaches.

c. *Bring the essentials:* Bring fishing equipment such as rods, reels, tackle, waders, and polarized sunglasses. Pack essentials such as sunscreen, bug repellent, and clothes suited for changeable weather conditions.

d. *Safety Precautions:* Prioritize safety while enjoying the fishing experience. Be wary of slippery rocks, fast-flowing water, and possible animal interactions. Always inform someone of your fishing intentions and planned return time.

e. *Environmental Respect:* Leave no trace and respect the clean natural surroundings. Dispose of rubbish correctly and avoid disturbing or damaging plants or animal habitats.

- **SKIING AND SNOWBOARDING**

Banff Ski Resorts: a. Banff Sunshine Village: Sunshine Village, located only 15 minutes from Banff town, provides a diversified terrain with 3,358 acres of skiable territory. It is known for its extended ski season, deep snow, and stunning vistas. The resort

Bruce Terry

offers runs for all ability levels, including beginner-friendly slopes and demanding bowls.

a. *Lake Louise Ski Resort:* Located in Banff National Park, Lake Louise Ski Resort is known for its breathtaking surroundings and diverse terrain. It has 4,200 skiable acres and can accommodate skiers at all ability levels. Lake Louise has something for everyone, from mild slopes for novices to exciting chutes and backcountry alternatives for expert riders.

b. *Mt. Norquay:* Just a short drive from Banff, Mt. Norquay is an ideal ski or snowboarding destination. It has a combination of groomed routes and steep, difficult terrain. Mt. Norquay is great for a short vacation or night skiing beneath the stars due to its proximity to town.

c. *Skiing and Snowboarding for All Skill Levels:* Banff's ski resorts provide a variety of routes for beginners, intermediates, and experienced riders. Each resort has specific learning areas with certified instructors who provide introductory courses to help you acquire confidence on the slopes. The resorts also include terrain parks with attractions for freestylers to show off their abilities.

d. *Beginners:* The beginning sections at Sunshine Village and Lake Louise are also superb, with mild slopes and dedicated instructional zones. To get started, lessons are provided, and rental stores have all of the essential equipment.

Bruce Terry

e. *Intermediates:* The Banff resorts provide a plethora of intermediate runs. Multiple blue runs in Sunshine Village's Goat's Eye Mountain and Lake Louise's Larch area provide the right combination of difficulty and fun.

f. *Experienced:* The Delirium Dive and Wild West zones at Sunshine Village are well-known for their difficult steep chutes and bowls for experienced skiers and snowboarders. Lake Louise has spectacular backcountry terrain, including the well-known Ptarmigan and Paradise Bowls.

- **MOUNTAIN BIKING**

Tracks & Terrain:

Banff National Park has a wide variety of mountain biking tracks to accommodate riders of all ability levels. From pleasant woodland roads to difficult technical descents, you'll discover trails that suit your needs. Among the most popular trails are:

a. *Tunnel Mountain walk:* This picturesque walk, ideal for novices, provides a moderate rise with excellent views of Banff townsite and surrounding mountains.

b. *Spray River circle:* This 19-kilometer circle offers spectacular vistas of the Spray River as well as modest hills and descents.

Bruce Terry

c. *Mount Norquay Trails:* Advanced riders may test their skills on Mount Norquay's technical trails, which are noted for their steep climbs, quick descents, and exhilarating features.

d. *Equipment & Rentals:* Don't worry if you don't have your mountain riding gear! There are various rental businesses in Banff where you may hire high-quality bikes, helmets, and safety gear. Banff Cycle, Snowtips-Bactrax, and Rebound Cycle are some of the most popular rental businesses. Make a reservation for your gear ahead of time, particularly during high tourist seasons.

Mountain biking may be a fun but physically challenging hobby. Keep the following safety considerations in mind to guarantee a safe and pleasurable experience:

a. Always wear a properly fitting helmet and consider other protection gear such as knee and elbow protectors.

b. *Know your limits:* Select trails that are appropriate for your skill level. Pushing oneself above your limits might result in accidents and injury.

c. *Bring necessary supplies:* Include a repair kit, extra water, food, and a first-aid kit. Before hitting the trails, make sure your bike is in excellent operating order.

Bruce Terry

d. Respect other trail users, yield to walkers and equestrians, and follow any posted trail regulations or closures.

Weather and Seasons:

Because the weather in Banff may be unpredictable, it's critical to check the forecast before your ride. With warmer temperatures and longer daylight hours, the summer months (June to September) provide the ideal riding conditions. However, be prepared for rapid weather changes and wear in layers at all times. Trails may be muddy or snow-covered in the spring and autumn, so verify trail conditions and closures before venturing out.

Banff provides guided tours and instruction whether you're new to mountain biking or want to explore the trails with an expert guide. These services may help you find the finest trails, develop your abilities, and learn about the area's flora, wildlife, and history.

Environmental Concerns: Banff National Park is home to a broad range of animals and fragile habitats. As a responsible mountain biker, you should try to reduce your environmental effect. Stay on approved paths, don't disturb animals, and pack away any rubbish or waste.

Nearby activities: While mountain biking may be the highlight of your vacation to Banff, don't overlook the area's other wonderful activities. Explore Lake Louise, take a swim in the Banff Upper Hot Springs, or savor local cuisine in the lovely town of Banff.

• CAMPING AND RVING

Choosing a Campground: Banff National Park has a variety of campsites that are suitable for both tent camping and RVing. Each campsite has its distinct characteristics, such as closeness to hiking trails, lakes, or picturesque overlooks. Tunnel Mountain, Two Jack Lakeside, Lake Louise, and Johnston Canyon are all popular Banff camping. Reservations are recommended since some campsites may fill up rapidly, particularly during high seasons.

Camping Equipment: If you want to camp, make sure you have all of the essential equipment. A nice tent, sleeping bags, a camping stove, cooking utensils, and portable chairs are all required. Pack warm clothes, rain gear, bug repellant, and a first-aid kit as well. Some campsites require bear-proof containers or bags to prevent animal interactions.

RVing in Banff: If you prefer the convenience of an RV, Banff has numerous RV-friendly campsites with amenities like power connections, water stations, and dump stations. Because some campsites have size limits, the size of your RV may limit your campground possibilities. RV campsites should be reserved well in advance, particularly during busy tourist seasons.

Bruce Terry

Exploring Banff National Park: Banff National Park is home to several natural marvels and attractions. Here are a few must-see attractions:

a. Lake Louise: This distinctive turquoise lake is surrounded by breathtaking mountain peaks and has spectacular hiking routes. The Lake Louise campsite is conveniently located near the lake.

b. Moraine Lake: A stunning glacial lake noted for its vibrant blue hue. Hike the Rockpile Trail for a 360-degree panorama of the lake and surrounding mountains.

c. Johnston Canyon: A popular hiking trail with spectacular waterfalls and tight limestone canyons. For easy access to the trailhead, stay at the Johnston Canyon campsite.

d. Peyto Lake: Peyto Lake, known for its unusual form and magnificent aquamarine hue, may be seen from a viewpoint along the Icefields Parkway.

e. Columbia Icefield: Take a guided tour or stroll on the Athabasca Glacier, one of Canada's greatest icefields.

Animal Safety:

Bears, elk, moose, and mountain goats are among the many species of animals found in Banff National Park. It is critical to practice animal safety and to keep human-wildlife contact to a minimum.

Bruce Terry

Food should be stored in bear-proof containers or lockers, rubbish should be disposed of correctly, and animals should be kept at a safe distance at all times. To guarantee a safe and responsible experience, familiarize yourself with Parks Canada's animal safety recommendations.

Hiking & Outdoor Activities:

Banff has a vast network of hiking paths ideal for hikers of all levels of expertise. There's something for everyone, from easy strolls to strenuous mountain excursions. Before beginning on any walk, make careful to verify trail conditions and weather predictions. Kayaking, canoeing, fishing, biking, and horseback riding are among more outdoor activities.

It Leave No Trace:

Is critical to respect and preserve the natural environment when camping and RVing in Banff. Follow the Leave No Trace guidelines, which include properly disposing of garbage, limiting campfire damage, respecting animals and plants, and remaining on authorized pathways.

Bruce Terry

CHAPTER 4

CULTURAL EXPERIENCES

- ### INDIGENOUS HERITAGE AND CULTURAL CENTERS

Why are Indigenous Heritage and Cultural Centers important?

Indigenous historical and cultural centers serve an important role in conserving, commemorating, and sharing Indigenous peoples' history, customs, and creative manifestations. Indigenous communities may present their art, music, dancing, storytelling, and culinary traditions at these sites. They are also valuable educational tools for tourists who want to learn more about the many cultures that have flourished in the Banff area for millennia.

Banff Park Museum National Historic Site: Begin your journey through Indigenous history by visiting the Banff Park Museum National Historic Site. This museum, which opened in 1903, has a magnificent collection of over 5,000 specimens of animals, birds, insects, and plants, as well as Indigenous artifacts.

Learn about the Indigenous connection with the land, hunting traditions, and traditional usage of natural resources on a guided tour. Learn about the remarkable relationship that exists between Indigenous peoples and the ecology of Banff National Park.

Bruce Terry

The Whyte Museum of the Canadian Rockies: is a must-see for anybody interested in the Indigenous cultures of the Canadian Rockies. The museum provides a comprehensive picture of the history, art, and cultural legacy of the Indigenous peoples who have occupied these regions for thousands of years via its numerous displays. Explore the Indigenous Gallery to see amazing artwork, crafts, and artifacts, as well as interact with interactive exhibits on Indigenous traditions and modern life.

Buffalo Nations Luxton Museum: Located in Banff, the Buffalo Nations Luxton Museum offers guests an interactive experience focusing on the Treaty 7 Nations' Indigenous history. The museum highlights the distinct cultures, traditions, and contributions of Indigenous peoples such as the Blackfoot, Blood, Peigan, Sarcee, and Stoney Nakoda. Discover engaging displays that emphasize these countries' history, spirituality, and aesthetic expressions, as well as their important role in defining the area.

Indigenous Artisan Market: If you want to meet Indigenous artists and craftsmen in person, go to the Indigenous Artisan Market. This bustling bazaar, which is often held in different Banff locales, features a diverse selection of traditional and modern Indigenous artwork, jewelry, clothes, and crafts. Engage in talks with the artists, learn about their cultural influences, and purchase one-of-a-kind and original souvenirs celebrating Indigenous history.

Bruce Terry

Participate in Cultural Events and Workshops: Look for cultural events and workshops conducted by Banff's Indigenous groups. Visitors may observe Indigenous rituals, dances, music performances, and storytelling sessions during these occasions. Workshops concentrating on traditional crafts like beading, drum making, and moccasin creation also provide hands-on experiences and opportunities to learn from Indigenous artists and cultural specialists.

- **BANFF CENTRE FOR ARTS AND CREATIVITY**

Location & Directions: The Banff Centre is located in Banff National Park, only a short drive from Banff. Calgary International Airport (YYC) is the closest major airport, located around 90 miles (145 kilometers) away. You may easily reach Banff by automobile, shuttle service, or bus from the airport. Alternatively, picturesque routes may be explored by taking a train or driving from other Canadian cities such as Edmonton or Vancouver.

Accommodation: The Banff Centre provides a range of lodging alternatives to meet the requirements of all visitors. You'll find pleasant and convenient housing on campus, ranging from charming hotel-style rooms to self-contained apartments. In addition, Banff town has a variety of hotels, lodges, and bed & breakfasts, giving guests more options.

Bruce Terry

Facilities and Amenities: The Banff Centre has cutting-edge facilities and amenities to enhance your creative experience. There are world-class theaters, music halls, art galleries, studios, rehearsal rooms, and digital media laboratories on the site. These rooms are used for a variety of creative disciplines such as visual arts, music, dance, theater, cinema, and others. There are also various food choices, a bookshop, exercise facilities, and lovely outdoor spots for leisure and inspiration on campus.

Programs and Workshops: The Banff Centre's vast variety of creative programs and workshops is one of its key draws. Renowned international artists, musicians, authors, and performers visit the Banff Centre to educate, collaborate, and inspire participants. The programs appeal to artists at all phases of their careers, ranging from short-term seminars to intensive residencies. Whether you're a novice or a seasoned professional, you'll find a chance to broaden your knowledge, explore new ideas, and network with like-minded people.

Events & Festivals: The Banff Centre presents a busy schedule of events and festivals throughout the year that highlight the abilities of its resident artists as well as visiting artists. There's always something exciting going on at the Banff Centre, from music concerts and theatrical performances to film screenings and literary readings. The Banff Summer Arts Festival, which features an

Bruce Terry

eclectic mix of performances and exhibits from numerous disciplines, is a highlight.

Outdoor leisure: In addition to creative activities, the Banff Centre's location in Banff National Park provides unequaled outdoor leisure options. Hiking, mountain biking, animal viewing, skiing, snowboarding, ice climbing, and other sports are available in the park. The beautiful vistas of the Canadian Rockies set the stage for adventure and discovery.

Exploring Banff: While staying at the Banff Centre, spend some time exploring the delightful town of Banff. Explore its charming streets, which are lined with boutique stores, art galleries, and restaurants serving a variety of cuisines. Visit the Banff Park Museum National Historic Site to learn about the area's fauna and natural heritage.

Sustainability and Conservation: The Banff Centre is dedicated to environmental stewardship and sustainability. As a visitor, you can help by respecting the natural environment, observing the park's rules, and engaging in eco-friendly activities. Programs at the Banff Centre also address environmental issues and foster innovative approaches to sustainability.

Bruce Terry

• BANFF PARK MUSEUMS

Why Visit the Museums in Banff National Park?

The Banff Park Museums are made up of two important institutions: the Banff Park Museum National Historic Site and the Buffalo Nations Luxton Museum. These museums augment the tourist experience by enabling them to dig into the various natural and cultural heritage of the Banff National Park region.

Banff Park Museum National Historic Site: Also known as the Banff Museum, the Banff Park Museum National Historic Site is a riveting overview of the region's fauna. Built-in 1903, the museum is an architectural jewel that combines Victorian charm with rustic beauty. Inside, visitors may expect to see more than 5,000 specimens of animals, birds, insects, and plants, including several endangered species.

The displays of the museum are expertly selected, offering a look into the natural richness of the Rockies. Lifelike taxidermy exhibits of notable creatures such as grizzly bears, elk, mountain goats, and wolves are available to visitors. The educational exhibits also teach visitors about the park's history, geological marvels, and attempts to conserve its unique environment.

Bruce Terry

Buffalo Nations Luxton Museum: The Buffalo Nations Luxton Museum is devoted to conserving and sharing the colorful culture and traditions of the Canadian Plains' First Nations peoples. This museum takes visitors on an interactive journey through the traditions, art, and tales of the region's Indigenous peoples, who have lived there for thousands of years.

The enormous collection of Indigenous items, including clothes, tools, and ceremonial objects, may be seen by visitors. The museum also conducts cultural performances, art exhibits, and interactive workshops to help visitors get a better knowledge of Indigenous culture and their strong relationship to the land.

Guided Tours and Educational Activities: Both museums provide guided tours as well as educational activities to improve the tourist experience. Knowledgeable guides give unique insights, stories, and scientific data to visitors, helping them to develop a greater knowledge of the exhibits and the region's history. These trips are a fantastic approach to properly understanding Banff National Park's cultural and environmental importance.

a. *Location:* The Banff Park Museums are ideally positioned in the center of Banff, making them readily accessible to tourists.

b. *Museum Hours*: Most museums are open from early morning to late afternoon, but check the official website for the most up-to-date information.

Bruce Terry

c. *Entry Fees:* Museums charge a modest entry price that goes toward the conservation and upkeep of the displays. Seniors, students, and families may be eligible for discounts.

d. *Accessible:* The museums seek to be inclusive, including wheelchair accessible as well as other facilities for visitors with special needs.

• CULTURAL EVENTS AND FESTIVALS

Banff Centre Mountain Film and Book Festival: The Banff Centre Mountain Film and Book Festival is one of the most well-known cultural events in Banff. This festival, held each November, promotes the spirit of outdoor adventure with a compelling mix of film screenings, book readings, panel discussions, and presentations. Visitors may immerse themselves in inspirational tales from mountaineers, adventurers, and filmmakers from all around the globe.

Banff Summer Arts Festival: The Banff Summer Arts Festival is a must-see for art lovers. This festival, which runs from June to August, features a wide variety of creative disciplines, including music, dance, theater, visual arts, and more. The Banff Centre for Arts and Creativity provides a variety of concerts, exhibits, and courses, giving new and renowned artists a platform to demonstrate their skills.

Bruce Terry

Banff Yoga Festival: The Banff Yoga Festival draws yogis from all over the world because it promotes health and awareness. This three-day event, held in May each year, provides a transforming experience via a mix of yoga lessons, seminars, meditation sessions, and wellness speeches. Participants may refresh their minds, body, and soul while taking in the breathtaking natural landscape of Banff.

Every year on July 1: Banff comes alive with patriotic enthusiasm to commemorate Canada's national day. The town transforms into a hive of celebrations, with parades, concerts, fireworks, and cultural acts. Visitors may immerse themselves in Canadian culture, sample local cuisine, and feel the love and friendliness of the Banff community.

Banff Winter Carnival: Banff's Winter Carnival has been a beloved tradition since the early twentieth century. This carnival celebrates the delights of winter with a variety of events such as ice carving contests, snowshoe races, dog sledding demonstrations, and more. Banff's streets are converted into a winter paradise, where tourists can indulge in seasonal goodies and soak in the festive ambiance.

Craft beer fans should mark their calendars for the Banff Craft Beer Festival, which is normally held in November. This event brings together brewers from around Canada and abroad, providing a chance to try a variety of craft beers and ciders. This event is a great

Bruce Terry

combination of tasty beverages, local cuisines, and companionship, with live music, food vendors, and a vibrant environment.

Whyte Museum of the Canadian Rockies Events: Throughout the year, the Whyte Museum of the Canadian Rockies, a cultural institution in Banff, organizes a variety of events and exhibits. The museum offers a platform for visitors to connect with Banff's rich past, from art exhibits that showcase the region's natural beauty to educational discussions and workshops on local history and indigenous cultures.

products, as well as an extensive wine selection. Their seasonal tasting menus allow you to sample the greatest delicacies of the area.

d. *Tooloulou's:* If you're craving Cajun and Creole food, go to Tooloulou's. This vibrant eatery provides traditional Louisiana cuisine with a Canadian touch. From jambalaya to po' boys, you'll discover a variety of rich and savory dishes that will take your taste senses on a journey.

e. *Park Distillery Restaurant and Bar:* Park Distillery Restaurant and Bar offers a one-of-a-kind eating experience. They not only provide a fantastic menu of Canadian comfort cuisine, but they also distill their alcohol on-site. Craft cocktails, wood-fired pizzas, and a pleasant atmosphere make it a favorite location for both residents and visitors.

- **SHOPPING IN BANFF**

Banff Avenue: Banff Avenue is the major road and retail district of Banff. This lively boulevard is dotted with stores, boutiques, and galleries, making it a shopaholic's dream. Visitors may buy anything from outdoor gear and apparel to one-of-a-kind gifts and souvenirs here. The street has a mix of well-known brands, small companies, and specialty shops. Banff Avenue is a wonderful spot to roam and explore, soaking in the mountain scenery while exploring the varied retail selections.

Bruce Terry

Cascade Plaza and Sundance Mall: Cascade Plaza and Sundance Mall are two retail complexes on Banff Avenue that provide a diverse selection of businesses. Fashion boutiques, jewelry stores, art galleries, and other businesses may be found in these complexes. Popular companies, including outdoor gear experts, as well as locally made artwork and jewelry, may be found here. Cascade Plaza and Sundance Mall provide consumers wishing to browse a range of retailers with a convenient and concentrated location.

Banff Farmer's Market: For those interested in sampling local vegetables and handcrafted crafts, the Banff Farmer's Market is a must-see. The market, which is held every Wednesday from June to September, has a variety of fresh fruits and vegetables, artisanal cheeses, baked delicacies, and handcrafted crafts. This bustling market allows visitors to connect with local merchants and learn about the region's agricultural history. It's a fantastic chance to buy one-of-a-kind souvenirs, try local delicacies, and support local manufacturers.

Native Arts and Crafts: Banff is situated on Indigenous peoples' traditional territory, and the town reflects this rich cultural past. Those looking for real Native arts and crafts may visit specialist stores that display and sell Indigenous artwork, jewelry, and traditional crafts. These shops often deal with Indigenous artists directly, guaranteeing fair trade practices and benefiting local

Bruce Terry

communities. Visitors may appreciate and maintain the region's cultural heritage by buying Native arts and crafts.

Banff Avenue Marketplace: The Banff Avenue Marketplace, located in the center of Banff, provides an amazing shopping experience. This indoor retail area has a variety of businesses such as fashion boutiques, specialized shops, and gift shops. It is an excellent location for finding one-of-a-kind apparel, accessories, souvenirs, and local artwork. The marketplace offers a convenient and weather-resistant shopping environment, making it an excellent choice regardless of the season.

Galleries and Artisans: Banff is a mecca for artists and art lovers alike. The town has a thriving art culture, with several galleries and studios displaying a wide spectrum of creative genres. Visitors may discover paintings, sculptures, photographs, and other types of visual art made by local and international artists by exploring these galleries. There are also several seminars and demonstrations where visitors may learn about different creative methods and even make their masterpieces.

- **SOUVENIRS AND LOCAL CRAFTS**

Banff Avenue: The primary retail district in town, lined with a profusion of shops, galleries, and specialty businesses. Visitors may browse a selection of stores selling a range of local crafts and gifts. Look for shops like The Banff Indian Trading Post, which sell real

Bruce Terry

Indigenous products including artwork, jewelry, and traditional attire. Another must-see is the Cascade Gift Shop, which has a large selection of goods, including locally manufactured ceramics, fabrics, and artwork.

The Whyte Museum of the Canadian Rockies: located on Banff Avenue, is not only a treasure mine of history and culture but also a terrific site to explore local crafts. The museum's gift store sells a variety of handmade products made by local craftsmen, including ceramics, woodwork, and jewelry. These crafts often reflect the region's natural beauty and tradition, making them great keepsakes of your Banff experience.

Banff Farmers' Market: If you visit Banff during the summer, make sure to visit the Banff Farmers' Market. This bustling market, held every Wednesday, highlights the abilities of local artists, craftsmen, and manufacturers. Handmade items such as artwork, leather products, fabrics, and much more may be found here. The market is a fantastic chance to engage with the designers and learn about the motivation behind their work.

Native Arts & Crafts: The indigenous culture in and around Banff is rich and varied, and you may discover true Native arts and crafts in several locations. The Buffalo Nations Luxton Museum has an extensive collection of artifacts and artworks, as well as a gift store selling handcrafted goods by indigenous artisans from the area.

Bruce Terry

Furthermore, the Bear Street Gallery and the Elk & Avenue Hotel Indigenous Gift Shop are worth visiting for their unique assortment of indigenous products, including sculptures, beading, and traditional attire.

The Banff Craft Market: The Banff Craft Market, located in the Cascade Gardens, is a treasure trove for craft aficionados. This market features the work of over 70 local craftsmen, who present a variety of crafts such as ceramics, jewelry, photography, and textiles. The market has a varied selection of classic and modern objects, guaranteeing that there is something to suit every taste and inclination.

Bruce Terry

88 BANFF TRAVEL GUIDE 2023-2024

CHAPTER 6

PRACTICAL INFORMATION

• SAFETY TIPS AND GUIDELINES

Study and Planning:

Before traveling to Banff, do an extensive study on the area, including weather conditions, trail difficulty levels, and any possible risks. Check the Parks Canada website for the most recent information, trail closures, and safety warnings. Plan your activities appropriately, taking into account your degree of physical condition and the experience necessary for each journey.

Weather Awareness: The weather in Banff may be unpredictable, and conditions can change quickly. Dress in layers, wear proper clothes, and have a waterproof and windproof outer layer on hand at all times. Even in the summer, be prepared for abrupt temperature changes, rain, or snow. Check the weather forecast daily and avoid going outside during severe weather warnings or stormy conditions.

Hiking and Outdoor Activities:

Select paths Appropriate to Your Skill Level: Banff National Park has a variety of hiking paths to suit all fitness levels and experience levels. Choose paths that are appropriate for your ability and be prepared for the mileage, elevation gain, and difficulty involved.

Bruce Terry

Notify Others: Before embarking on a trek, notify someone trustworthy of your intentions, including the route name, expected return time, and emergency contact numbers. This guarantees that someone is aware of your surroundings and may seek assistance if necessary.

Carry Necessary Equipment: Wear durable, comfortable hiking footwear with enough ankle support and traction.

Carry a comprehensive map compass, or GPS device with you to help you remain on course.

Food and drink: Bring enough food and drink to last you the whole journey.

Keep a well-stocked first aid kit with necessities such as bandages, antiseptics, and pain medications.

Carry a whistle to signal for assistance in the event of an emergency.

Bear Spray: If you want to go bear hunting, bring bear spray and learn how to use it properly.

Wildlife Protection: Maintain a Safe Distance: Always respect nature and stay a safe distance from animals. For improved viewing, use binoculars or telephoto lenses.

Feeding animals is prohibited and may result in deadly interactions.

Bruce Terry

Bear Safety: If you come into contact with a bear, be calm, back away gently, and never run. Follow Parks Canada's bear interaction rules.

Water Safety: Banff is well-known for its beautiful lakes, rivers, and waterfalls. Follow these safety measures while participating in aquatic activities:

Swim Only in specified locations: Only swim in specified locations and obey any posted signs or cautions.

Wear Life Jackets: Always wear a properly fitting life jacket or personal flotation device while boating, kayaking, or canoeing.

Be Wary of Currents: Rivers and bodies of water may have powerful currents. Swimming in unknown places with strong currents or undertows should be avoided.

Highway Safety:

If you want to explore Banff by automobile, take the following precautions:

Follow Traffic Rules: Pay attention to speed restrictions and road signs. Keep an eye out for animals crossing the road, particularly at dawn and night?

Bruce Terry

Preventing Wildlife Collisions: Use care while driving in wildlife-prone locations. Maintain vigilance, particularly at night, and use your high lights when there is no incoming traffic.

Winter Driving: Carry snow chains, utilize winter tires, and check road conditions before going in the winter. Be prepared for ice and snowy situations by following winter driving instructions.

• HEALTH AND MEDICAL SERVICES

It is important to examine the health and medical services available while planning a vacation to Banff, a lovely town set in the heart of the Canadian Rockies. While Banff is renowned for its breathtaking scenery and outdoor experiences, it is important to focus on your health and well-being during your trip. This complete guide will offer you detailed information on Banff's health and medical facilities, guaranteeing a safe and healthy trip.

Health Care:

Banff has several health care facilities that serve both inhabitants and tourists. These clinics provide a variety of medical services, ranging from general care to specialty therapies. Banff's significant health facilities include:

a. *Banff Mineral Springs Hospital:* Banff Mineral Springs Hospital, located at 305 Lynx Street, is the region's principal healthcare center. It provides emergency treatment, acute care, laboratory tests, radiography, and general medical consultations. The hospital employs highly qualified healthcare workers and is prepared to address a broad variety of medical conditions.

b. *Primary Care Clinics:* Numerous primary care clinics in Banff provide routine medical services, vaccinations, and preventive care. These clinics serve both locals and tourists and are great non-emergency medical options. The Banff Medical Clinic and the Banff Community Health Centre are two noteworthy clinics in Banff.

Banff is well-equipped to give prompt aid in the event of a medical emergency. The following are the key emergency services in the area:

c. *Banff Mineral Springs Hospital Emergency Department*: The Banff Mineral Springs Hospital emergency department is open 24 hours a day, seven days a week, and provides fast and specialist treatment for serious medical conditions. It is manned by competent emergency medical experts who are trained to address a wide range of crises.

d. *Ambulance Services*: In the event of a medical emergency, phone 911 to contact Banff's ambulance service. To guarantee prompt transportation and the provision of first medical treatment, the ambulance service works closely with the local hospital.

Bruce Terry

d. *Pharmacies:* Numerous pharmacies in Banff sell prescription pharmaceuticals, over-the-counter medications, and basic health supplies. These pharmacies have certified pharmacists on staff who can help with medication-related questions. Shoppers Drug Mart and Rexall Pharmacy are two famous pharmacies in Banff.

e. *Travel Insurance:* Comprehensive travel insurance is highly recommended while visiting Banff or any other location. If necessary, travel insurance may cover medical bills, emergency medical evacuation, and repatriation. If you want to partake in outdoor activities such as hiking or skiing during your vacation, be sure your insurance coverage covers them.

Outdoor Safety:

The unspoiled nature and outdoor activities in Banff have inherent dangers. Prioritize your safety by following the instructions below:

a. Plan and prepare your activities ahead of time, taking into account your physical ability and weather circumstances.

b. Stay hydrated and bring enough food and drink for long outdoor trips.

c. Dress for the weather and use proper footwear to prevent injury.

d. Carry a first-aid kit with all required materials, such as bandages, antibacterial ointments, and any prescription prescriptions.

Bruce Terry

• CURRENCY AND BANKING FACILITIES

The official currency of the nation is the Canadian Dollar (CAD). The currency is issued in banknotes and coins, with banknotes ranging in amounts from $5 to $100. 5 cents (nickel), 10 cents (dime), 25 cents (quarter), $1 (loonie), and $2 (toonie) coins are available. It is best to have Canadian dollars with you while visiting Banff since most local establishments accept cash payments. Major credit cards, on the other hand, are generally accepted in most businesses.

Money Exchange: If you need to exchange your money for Canadian dollars, Banff has various possibilities. Banks and credit unions provide currency exchange services, albeit their rates are not always the best. You may also use money exchange services offered by private exchange offices or kiosks, which are often available in prominent tourist regions. Although these private exchange offices may provide reasonable rates, it is critical to evaluate rates and fees before making any swaps.

Banking Services: Banff has various banks and financial organizations that provide a variety of banking services to inhabitants and tourists alike. Royal Bank of Canada (RBC), Toronto-Dominion Bank (TD), Bank of Montreal (BMO), and Canadian Imperial Bank of Commerce (CIBC) are the most notable banks in Canada. These banks have Banff branches and provide services including currency exchange, cash withdrawals, and deposits.

ATMs: ATMs are readily accessible around Banff and enable you to withdraw cash in Canadian dollars with your debit or credit card. The majority of ATMs accept major international credit cards including Visa, Mastercard, and American Express. However, it is best to verify with your bank or card issuer about any possible international transaction fees or card use restrictions when abroad.

Credit and debit cards: are accepted frequently in Banff, including hotels, restaurants, stores, and tourist attractions. Visa and Mastercard are the most often accepted cards, followed by American Express and Discover, which may be accepted in limited quantities. It is usually a good idea to notify your credit card issuer of your trip intentions to prevent any possible card authorization complications.

Most ATMs accept debit cards connected to major international networks, such as Plus or Cirrus, for cash withdrawals. It is, however, essential to verify with your bank about any international transaction fees or daily withdrawal limitations.

While Banff is typically a secure place, it is prudent to take steps to safeguard your money and personal information. ATMs should be used in well-lit and busy places, ideally those adjacent to bank offices. Use caution while using ATMs that seem suspicious or show evidence of tampering. When making card payments, keep

Bruce Terry

your card visible and make sure the transaction is completed in your presence.

It is also advisable to keep a variety of payment methods on hand, such as cash and credit cards, to ensure you have backup choices in case of problems or crises.

• COMMUNICATION AND INTERNET ACCESS

Mobile Network Coverage: Banff has good mobile network coverage, which allows for smooth connection across much of the town and surrounding regions. Rogers, Bell, and Telus are among the major Canadian telecommunications carriers with excellent service in Banff. Before your journey, check your provider's coverage map to guarantee compatibility with the available networks in the area.

Internet connectivity: Most hotels, resorts, and lodges in Banff provide internet connectivity to their visitors. The majority of lodgings provide free Wi-Fi in their rooms, lobbies, and common spaces. However, it is usually a good idea to clarify the availability and quality of internet services with your selected hotel before making a reservation.

Public Wi-Fi Hotspots: Banff also has public Wi-Fi hotspots located around the town. Public Wi-Fi services are normally available on

Bruce Terry

Banff Avenue, the main thoroughfare, and the center area. Visitors may also use free Wi-Fi in the Banff Public Library and various restaurants, cafés, and retail areas. Keep in mind that public Wi-Fi networks may not provide the same level of security and privacy as private networks, so use care while doing sensitive activities on them.

Internet Cafes: If you need a dedicated workplace or access to computers, Banff has a few internet cafes. For a price, these organizations often provide high-speed internet connections, computer rentals, and printing services. Check local directories or ask your lodging for ideas on nearby internet cafés.

Mobile Data and SIM Cards: If you want to use the internet while on the road, you may get a local SIM card for your smartphone or mobile device. In Canada, there are various mobile network operators, and their services are available in Banff. Consider getting a prepaid SIM card from a carrier like Rogers, Bell, or Telus, which provide a variety of data options to fit your requirements. Check that your device is unlocked and compatible with the Canadian network frequency bands.

Internet Access in National Parks: Banff National Park, which includes Banff, has stunning natural vistas. It is crucial to remember, however, that internet service inside the park may be restricted or non-existent in certain regions. While certain facilities, such as

Bruce Terry

tourist centers and campsites, may provide Wi-Fi, it is often more restricted than the services provided by the municipality. Take advantage of this chance to unplug and truly immerse yourself in the park's spectacular splendor.

• VISITORS INFORMATION CENTERS

The significance of visitor information centers:

Information and Direction: Visitors Information Centers are a one-stop shop for detailed information on Banff. These centers give reliable and up-to-date information about hiking routes, animal viewing spots, camping grounds, and local attractions. The staff is well-trained and can provide helpful insights and suggestions customized to your interests, ensuring that you get the most out of your stay in Banff.

Maps and Brochures: Banff's Visitors Information Centers provide a large range of maps and brochures to help you plan your trip. These sites give in-depth information on the area, such as attractions, lodging, food alternatives, and leisure activities. With these tools in hand, you may easily tour Banff and find lesser-known hidden treasures.

Assistance with vacation Planning: Planning a vacation to Banff may be difficult, particularly for first-time guests. Visitors Information Centers provide individualized advice to assist you in

Bruce Terry

planning an itinerary that meets your tastes and time restrictions. Whether you want to explore hiking trails, beautiful drives, or cultural activities, the staff can recommend the finest alternatives and provide tips on how to make the most of your time.

Banff National Park is home to a broad range of animals, including bears, elk, mountain goats, and bighorn sheep. Visitors Information Centers play an important role in teaching tourists about wildlife safety, ensuring that visitors understand how to watch and interact with the animals appropriately. They give information on animal viewing sites, interaction best practices, and any particular rules in place to protect both tourists and wildlife.

Banff Visitor Information Centers:

Banff Visitor Centre: Located on Banff Avenue in the center of Banff, the Banff Visitor Centre is the principal information center for tourists. You'll find a plethora of materials here, such as brochures, maps, and knowledgeable personnel that can answer your inquiries. The center also has informative exhibits and displays that provide visitors with an understanding of Banff's natural and cultural history.

Lake Louise Visitor Centre: This facility, located near the famed Lake Louise, is a must-see for tourists touring the Lake Louise region. It provides regional information such as trail maps, activity suggestions, and information on the magnificent Moraine Lake. The

Bruce Terry

experts at the center can help you organize your trip, give safety advice, and make the most of your stay.

Banff National Park Information Centre: Located near the park's western entrance, this information center is an ideal starting place for tourists. It informs visitors about park laws, route conditions, and camping possibilities. The center also has exhibits and interactive displays that highlight the park's diverse ecosystems and conservation initiatives.

Bow Valley Parkway Visitor Centre: This facility, located along the gorgeous Bow Valley Parkway, caters exclusively to travelers visiting the Bow Valley area. It provides details about animal observation sites, picnic spaces, and hiking paths. The center is an excellent visit for anyone interested in viewing wildlife since it gives information on current sightings as well as wildlife photography advice.

Bruce Terry

CONCLUSION

In conclusion, the Banff Travel Guide for the years 2023-2024 presents a thorough and detailed overview of one of the most compelling places in the world. Banff, nestled in the heart of the Canadian Rockies, continues to amaze guests with its beautiful vistas, plentiful wildlife, and unrivaled outdoor activities.

The book contains a broad variety of information, including crucial travel suggestions, hotel alternatives, eating recommendations, and must-visit sights. With a concentration on both summer and winter activities, it appeals to all sorts of tourists, from adventure junkies seeking exhilarating encounters to nature lovers wishing for calm.

The guide stresses the preservation of Banff's natural beauty and advocates sustainable tourist practices. It underlines the significance of respecting the environment, animals, and local populations. Visitors are advised to visit the national park carefully and leave little harm, protecting its pristine status for future generations.

With the inclusion of up-to-date information on hiking paths, skiing chances, animal spotting places, and beautiful overlooks, the book provides a complete resource for guests planning their Banff vacation. It gives essential insights into lesser-known treasures, hidden gems, and off-the-beaten-path experiences, enabling visitors to explore the region's genuine spirit.

Bruce Terry

Furthermore, the book emphasizes the range of interests and preferences among tourists, advising on varied budgets and travel types. From luxury resorts and gourmet dining experiences to budget-friendly lodgings and informal restaurants, it caters to a broad spectrum of interests and budgets.

As Banff continues to expand and adapt to the changing demands of guests, the book offers a vital reference for navigating the region's dynamic tourism sector. It welcomes the newest changes in the region, such as new trails, attractions, and cultural events, ensuring that tourists have access to the most relevant and accurate information.

In summary, the Banff Travel Guide for 2023-2024 gives visitors the tools and information essential to organize an outstanding vacation to one of the world's most awe-inspiring places. By integrating practical knowledge with an appreciation for Banff's natural treasures, the book inspires visitors to explore, interact, and connect with this intriguing corner of the Canadian Rockies.

Made in United States
North Haven, CT
26 January 2024